What Was Not Said

Echoes From The Holocaust

SEAN M. TEAFORD

authorHOUSE®

AuthorHouse™
1663 Liberty Drive
Bloomington, IN 47403
www.authorhouse.com
Phone: 1 (800) 839-8640

Published by AuthorHouse 02/02/2016

ISBN: 978-1-5049-7674-9 (sc)
ISBN: 978-1-5049-7675-6 (e)

Library of Congress Control Number: 2016901794

Print information available on the last page.

This book is printed on acid-free paper.

For the millions of voices lost
— we will never forget.

Acknowledgements

The author would like to thank the following people: Melissa Frederick, Dan Sklar, Harris Gardner, and Rhina Espaillat for their input and editorial work. Samuel Hazo, Robert Pinsky, James Chichetto, Charles Fishman, and Elie Wiesel for their kind encouragement and endorsements. Eileen D'Angelo (along with all of the other Mad Poets), Sara Quay (and the Endicott College community), Rabbi Avi Winokur, and Rabbi Alan Iser for their support in writing these poems. Mom and Dad for supporting my decision to pursue my poetic potential. And, of course, my wife Samantha for pushing me to keep writing through the tough times. These works would have never been possible without the help and support of these individuals.

Grateful acknowledgement is given to the editors of the following anthology and magazines in which these poems have appeared (or will be appearing): *Midstream Magazine*: "A Hundred Stars" (first published as "The Lost Generation") and "With His Children"; *The Endicott Review*: "Chosen Steps" and "Without His Mother to Light the Candles"; *The Hypertexts* (www.thehypertexts.com): "Warsaw Epidemic", "Door to Door and Back", "Children's Games", "With His Children", and "A Pure Breath"; and Blood to Remember: American Poets on the Holocaust: "Warsaw Epidemic" and "A Pure Breath".

Other Works By Sean M. Teaford

Teaching A Stone To Talk: Nature Poems (Bending Tree Press, 2003)
Kaddish Diary (Pudding House Publications, 2005)
Paintings In Under A Thousand Words (Author House, 2016)

Contents

Preface

I originally set out reading these memoirs for the sake of learning about the history and experiences of the Holocaust. As I read further into these books I came to an astonishing realization that they are not historic texts... they are scripts of life's dark side.

These are pages in our story that some may gloss over and feel that they have missed nothing but those of us who have read these pages will never forget our life as one people; we will always remember the blood with which those words were scribed and we know that those who were murdered are not a footnote. They are the ones who will forever be our teachers. These poems will never be more than an echo of their whispers.

****

The Holocaust is a subject all of us are aware of but there are countless accounts that are seldom heard. Based on diaries, letters, memoirs, etc. of the Holocaust, this series of poems describe the life surrounding these writings. The result is a historical fiction account of what might have happened.

During the winter of 2004, I began writing about the Holocaust because I needed an outlet for my own pain and fear. It was not a conscious decision to write about Janusz Korczak, it just happened. I began relating to Korczak and his children on the most basic level: I was dejected, I couldn't eat, and I was in pain. It was a time in my life when writing was work.

I was struck not only with what Korczak recorded in his diary but also by the thoughts of what was not written in those pages. This feeling was intensified further when I would come across passages that were of longing, passages that recalled of a different time in Korczak's life, a time without worry. I understood the feeling of wanting to escape but my thoughts were firmly planted in the Warsaw orphanage in which Korczak was writing amongst sleeping children.

It was the contrariness between thought and reality that forced me to scribe ink on the page. Korczak wrote, "I used to write at stops, in a meadow under a pine tree, sitting on a stump. Everything seemed important and if I did not note it down I would forget. An irretrievable loss to humanity."

I couldn't stop thinking about what the children were experiencing at that time, at that exact moment. Were they awake or asleep, were they hungry, were they scared, were they healthy or sick? What was happening outside the window, what sounds did they hear, what smells slipped through the cracks?

I knew the setting of the poem and so I began with the first two stanzas:

> The sun peeled the
> gray from clouds,
> burning their pewter lining.
>
> Mid-day February and
> sick students were having
> troubled afternoon naps.

After completing these six lines I was stuck. I knew I didn't have enough information to continue; I knew I didn't have the experiential or emotional ammunition to finish the poem.

I began by researching the Warsaw Ghetto, by studying texts and maps, as well as watching documentary footage and listening to the testimonies of Holocaust survivors who had lived in the Ghetto.

But that was not enough. I had to remember what it was like to feel helpless, to feel sick, to be in pain, to be hungry.

My dejection and pain contributed to my research and the resulting sickness and inability to eat from the intensity of the pain helped me to understand the constancy of their feelings.

> Their dry heaves echoed
> in the doctor's ears-- he had
> nothing to cure a cough,
> no antidote for a fever.
> The flu flooded the ghetto
> like a forgotten fog.
>
> The children lay tightly
> curled in their cots-- they
> lay pale, restlessly immobile.
> With every turning groan,
> their clothes ruffled like wet paper.

The poem was beginning to become personal; my experiences were starting to become their experiences but the raw emotions were missing.

Emotionally, I had to force myself to relive the deaths of two uncles, three friends, and the man that was the closest thing I had to a grandfather. I remembered seeing them lying there, silent, distant. I had to relive these experiences every day, numerous times during each day, to feel the consistency and never ending feeling of loss before I was able to continue writing. I was exhausted by the time I continued writing...

> Some orphans cried but
> nobody made a sound.
> Many prayers are silent.

The turn was established and I felt that I was able to understand, at a basic level, what their experience was like. I knew there was something missing from the picture but, at the time, I could not write another line.

A few days later, the elusive piece of the puzzle was revealed to me when I woke up to sounds of people talking as they sipped coffee below my apartment window. As I recalled the physical and emotional tools I had acquired prior, I wrote the final two stanzas:

> Below the venting glass
> panes, standing on the sleet
> encrusted sidewalk, soldiers
> laughed while slurping soup-
> Korczak's stomach twisted
> as he heard uneaten broth
> splash and sizzle in the snow.
>
> The fragrant steam slid
> through cracked windows;
> he listened as his children
> sniffed and moaned. He had
> no bowls to scrape with
> spoons they did not possess.

I continued reading Korczak's diary and ideas for poems did not stop with the completion of this one, twelve more poems followed (and dozens about Hertha Fiener and Filip Muller), the writing process becoming easier with every new poem. However, the resulting nightmares and emotional exhaustion increasingly got worse; I continued to relive not only my own past but the Holocaust as well.

This is not just the story of Holocaust victims but mine as well as yours; these poems are what was not said. This collection fills in the colors of the outlines presented in these Holocaust accounts. I hope that you will find these poems not only stirring but accurate as well. I want people to hear these stories, I want to give these people a voice, and I only hope that my whispered words are enough.

Introduction

Every memoir has something missing. This is not a conscious decision by the author; it is simply the perspective of the writer filtered through the impermanence of memory. Sometimes it's a forgotten foreshadowing phrase said in passing or simply what is happening outside when their focus is on the room in which they are sitting. These are the aspects painted in this collection.

Divided into three sections, this collection fills in the details absent from these Holocaust memoirs.

> I: Hertha Feiner
> Hertha Feiner was a divorced (from a gentile) mother of two daughters, Inge and Marion. Hertha was a teacher in a Jewish day school in Berlin before the Nazi's came to power. She taught until she was forced to work elsewhere (she was later assigned by the SS to type the deportation lists). Feiner's passion was teaching her students but her love was for her daughters whom she had sent to boarding school in Gland, Switzerland (Les Reyons) to save them from the Nazi's inevitable atrocities. Hertha wrote to her daughters as frequently as she could – many of these letters were collected in the book <u>Before Deportation: Letters from a Mother to Her Daughters: January 1939 – December 1942</u> (Northwestern University Press: Evanston (IL), 1999). Feiner committed suicide while on a train making its way to Auschwitz.
> II: Janusz Korczak
> Janusz Korczak was an elderly doctor who cared for countless children at an orphanage in the Warsaw Ghetto. Born Henryk Goldzmit in 1878, Korczak first

made a name for himself in Poland as a pediatrician, writer, and children's rights advocate. Korczak would later change his name to shield himself from the growing anti-Semitism of the time. He wrote autobiographical novels at the turn of the century as well as founding the first children's newspaper, *The Little Review*, and he had a radio program as "the Old Doctor." Later, he gave up his medical practice to establish the first progressive orphanages in Warsaw. From that point until the beginning of the Nazi occupation of Warsaw, Korczak wrote about children and for children. Korczak was 64 when he began writing Ghetto Diary (Yale University Press: New Haven (CT), 2003). Refusing numerous attempts at freedom, Korczak died with his children at Treblinka.

III: Filip Müller

Deported from Sered, Czechoslovakia, Filip Muller (#29236) worked for three years as a prisoner in the "Sonderkommando" in the gas chambers and crematoria of Auschwitz. Every day he saw the flames extinguished of many, now forgotten, candles. Frequently writing notes about his experiences, Müller spent years after his liberation trying to educate all those who would listen to his account but he did not compile and publish his testimony until 1970 under the title Eyewitness Auschwitz: Three Years in the Gas Chambers (Ivan R. Dee, Publishers: Chicago (IL), 1979). Müller has lived in Western Europe since 1969.

The moments of silence between their recorded actions, these poems, are merely the wind that carries the ash across our eyes and nose.

I

Hertha Feiner

The Visit: July 1939

"I'm so glad that you like being there, in a peaceful environment that makes studying fun. If I could only get a glimpse of you!" – Hertha Feiner

Pen and paper lay
abandoned, books
remained stacked
across the shelves.

No letters or lessons
for three weeks.

Berlin wilted in a sweltering
summer slumber; Germany
set its war clock for two months.

Inge and Marion were
passengers on the train
from Switzerland –
their mother waited.

Hours passed until time
arrested with the hiss
of the arriving train.

As her schoolchildren
were paroled from studies,
Hertha embraced her
daughters in the belly
of the whale – smoke filled
their lungs before the purge.

All decrees forgotten;
laws twisted and bruised;
religions, countries,
and politics refused
to divide. Life was
basic in the love of a
mother and her daughters.

Summer Vacation

*"Our vacation starts on Friday, and you can imagine how sad I am
that you're not going to be here... And I will probably have to stay here
since I don't know where else to go. Maybe I'll still find something." –
Hertha Feiner*

The students sat still
in their seats staring
at the window as summer
steamed the glass.

The students had been
grated over the year
with a decade's worth
of fervor. Their naivety
in chains, they no longer
had the freedom
of childhood— their thoughts
deliberately dictated
in weathered voices.

Thunder growled
like a guard dog—
their feet shuddered
without hesitation.

The year was consumed;
they feared the
repercussions of the
charred summer.

Feiner had no lessons that
would prepare the children.

Transition

"I am firmly convinced that you would behave quite differently toward me if you knew exactly what the situation here is. I am often very sad and depressed; your letters would be the best remedy for lifting my spirits, but I wait in vain." – Hertha Feiner

Hertha felt the earth exhale as
Pearl peered from below
her black hair and asked,
"Ms. Feiner, why does God hate us?
Why does God want us to die?"

Feiner was furious— pierced
with obsidian sorrow and
hatred of ones who programmed
Pearl's life and had shaped
the little girl's doubts of God.
She never knew propaganda
could have this effect.

Hertha broadly inhaled settling
chalk dust and composed
her quivering voice,
"God wants you to taste every
moment and let it linger
on your tongue. Your kaddish
will not be recited until
years after I have passed."

A cynical grin seized the young
girl's porcelain cheeks.

Before her students were set free
for the day, Hertha whispered
to the class from below
her hidden tears,
"That is the only lesson
I wish you would never abandon.
Never forget what I have just said."

Time to Think

"We don't want to believe that the time might come when I would not hear from you or you from me, but as long as we still have the chance, let's write to each other as often and in as much detail as possible." – Hertha Feiner

Absence filled the void
where Mutti awaited
an update from her daughters.
Her memories began to
wander during her brisk
dusk walk back home.

Grass pressed through a crack
only to be stamped against
concrete and bruised
under Hertha's bare foot.

All Jewish schools in Berlin
lay in rubble; pages scattered
from shredded books.

Her student's thoughts chipped
with every shovel of snow.
Her new appointment stagnated,
weighted by official neglect;
her lessons left to rust
under worried sweat.

The routine of sleep now tedious
and exhaustion common,
thoughts of her daughters'
peaceful slumber uncoiled
her crippled nerves.

Mailing Letters

"I'm gradually getting used to this different way of life. Today I had a good rest, and that makes the world look a little rosier." – Hertha Feiner

Hertha walked swiftly
to the post office, eyes
tracing the trickle of the gutter.

The dogs that devoured
Jezebel were now trained
and prodded to attack
those who did not comply—
the city, in SS eyes,
now the open field.

Sparks of scraping shovels
singed her bare legs as her
shoes soaked in gray slush.

Spilled grammar tests
woven like inked marble
in six-foot drifts.
She never had time
to pass them back.

The corner of the stamp
flapped in the breeze
of a slamming door.

Finally, the envelope was sealed;
its contents, stamped by the censors,
had passed inspection.

Walking to Work Monday Morning

"I am sad not to be with my schoolchildren anymore, even more so because they now have a teacher who is over sixty and does not like teaching. I didn't even say good-bye to the children, since I was dismissed on Sunday and my new work began on Monday at 7:00 A.M." – Hertha Feiner

Her lips lay level,
the corners of her mouth
tilted toward the ground.

Wet hair glazed her face
as sweat and snow
froze her expression.

She had seen the last
of her students and her
bloodshot eyes squinted
with every prick
from crystallized tears.

All of her lessons
would now be in letters
to her daughters.

But, later, she would
once again decide
who passes,
who stays,
who will
continue
learning.

A New Daily Routine

"Our circle of friends is slowly getting smaller. Your former teacher Mr. Neufeld died; he committed suicide. In recent weeks he looked so terrible, you would scarcely have recognized him... Oh, if only things would change soon!" – Hertha Feiner

Absent of a single school bell rung,
the monotony of seasons passed
without a change in her routine.
Every morning, Hertha had to
convince herself to walk to work.

In the morning sun's yellow-orange
bleach she would pass road signs to
a city she no longer knew – an alien city.

The wind chime hung still
in the clinging August air.
Buildings lay in piles
like large ant hills.
Dust swirled from cracks in a jar
cradled in the rubble.

Just before the crest
of afternoon hours,
Hertha abandoned her new job
so she could try to recapture
the feeling she used to have
as she watched her students
in the school yard after lunch.

This, too, was shattered
into fragmented memory
when Hertha saw a rigid
man on the creased concrete.

His liquid light wove a web
across the sidewalk, his body
lay inert, silent at pedestrian feet.
The congealed pool reflected
the solar furnace, its fire burning
this image of extinguished life
into Hertha's swollen eyes.

Hertha realized— her only daily
decisions were hope and despair.

Seated at her desk, she
continued to emboss her
assigned pages of the Nazi script.

Her new life had her sentencing
her students to the permanence
of SS lists— she saw
her daughter's faces
in each name she typed.

Lamps and candles slowly began
to glow as dusk arrested day.

Not an hour had passed before
the veiled sky fell. Falling
through ashen clouds,
the rain was no longer pure.

The polluted rain pierced
the charcoal night
that writhed in silent pain.
The soot stained drops
erased nothing but the future.

Working for a New Berlin

"We are going through a very grave period here. This time Walter Matzdorff and many of my pupils are on the list [for deportation to Riga]. I have to work hard and try to help as many people as possible.' –
Hertha Feiner

The keys slowly clacked like a train
rolling on frost-bitten tracks.

Her eyes squinted to read another
list of names. Her lips repeated
the columns like prayers. Her touch
embossed the brittle pages.

Friends, neighbors, and room-mates
shackled from past and present
grazed the teacher's fingertips.

Hertha penned the pages,
their sentences announced
in the streets of Old Berlin;
she believed it was her
script that put them on the trains.

This labor kept her alive.
This is the job Mutti rarely
revealed to her daughters.

Remorse

"My one consolation is to know that you have a nice home and are happy, healthy, and content. I have never had many material possessions, but I know how infinitely rich I am because I have you and your love—and you have my undying mother's love." – Hertha Feiner

In the morning,
Hertha could hear
passionate murmurs
of the Mourner's Kaddish
from friends, neighbors,
and half-familiar faces.
It was the only conversation
they would have that morning.

The daily sorrow of life
knew no Saturday rest—
breaking Sabbath law
burdened her leaded steps.

Hertha wept whenever
she remembered the
stillness and silence
of her memory's Shabbat.

The Holiness of the day
remained hidden
under gunfire and
moans of the dying.

A Night Without a Letter

"I'm unhappy about many things, but more than anything it hurts to hear so rarely from you. True, people have come between us, but in spite of everything, we must not lose touch. Let's talk to one another again, the way we used to..." – Hertha Feiner

Hertha was meshugga le-davar
over her daughters. She softly
squeezed the patch on her dress
sewn by Inge and Marion.

Hertha had not been able to sleep
for what seemed like decades.

In the silhouette of body and bed,
muzzle flashes echoed – piercing
light across the divided city.
With singeing heat of darkness
and her vision blurred from tears,
she could no longer find their
faces on the back of her eye lids.

Shuddered from slumber,
her eyes were burdened by
the fragments of fractured night.

The stars shined bright
in the powerless night but upon
the breath of the sun they dimmed
to sparks of their former brilliance...
darkness in a Nazi city.

Like Moses gazing across the river
to the Promised Land, Hertha knew
she would not be a part
of her children's future—
Mutti could no longer be their guide.

A Final Lesson

*"Oh, if only everything were different! Your chairs here are always empty; will we ever again sit at our table together, having a cozy talk." –
Hertha Feiner*

Feiner's words rang in their ears—
informing them of her departure.
The children knew what
her shallow breaths meant.

Her students latched to her side
tighter than her own children—
her limbs numbed by their grasp.

She wrote to her daughters—
her train would soon be leaving;
but that was all she said.

Hertha wanted their memories to be
of a mother's strength and embrace;
branded thoughts of their final visit
before gray rain began to fall.

Painfully Numb

"Sometimes I think that my front door is about to open and you will come storming through, and then I am depressed because it was all just a fantasy." – Hertha Feiner

The Snow flowed
across broken stones,
churning above the rails
with every turning wheel.

Nail heads tore at
the soles of her shoes
as she was slowly
pushed up the ramp.

She was the last to
walk through
the cattle car doors.

Winter drifts jolted the car
around every turn –
she remained on her feet;
one of the few who could stand.

Gripped in her chapped
palm, the pill began to
dissolve in labored sweat.

Thoughts of her daughters
slowed her lips but her
tongue refused to mourn.
With disturbing comfort,
the pill slipped down her throat.

Before the last bitter breath
massaged her lungs,
she regretted not writing
one more letter.

The capsule exploded like
a shattered fountain pen.

As flakes of ice and ash swirled
in the breaths of parched whispers,
Mütterlein lay confined in
sleep's final iron embrace.

II

Janusz Korczak

Chosen Steps

"Whenever the stems of potato plants grew excessively, a heavy roller would be dragged over them to crush them so that the fruit in the ground could ripen better." – Janusz Korczak

The flowers wilted,
resting on soiled beds--
there was no food
for plant or child.
The children,
chosen by God,
lived on little more
than rotting air.

Most of them had fewer years
than points on their armbands.
They walked deliberately,
like old men, careful
not to leave the gutters.

In the orphanage, they
would press every square
with the same meticulous steps;
cautiously and steadily,
but with a different purpose.

Even absent of leather
to protect their soles;
with every barefoot stride,
their feet refused to blister.

Teaching His Children

"Everyone should know how to sketch in pencil what he wants to retain in memory. Not to be able to do that is to be illiterate." – Janusz Korczak

In a sadly stern low voice
the doctor pried
splintered ineloquence
from his parched throat.
King Matthew's words
failed to pass his tongue.

He was only able
to retain their attention
for an hour each day.
The children were getting older;
they were now the orators
telling one another stories.
Accounts they told
were without morals--
they were the recited
records of the ghetto.

Korczak knew he was slowly
losing his children.

Before occupation, the children
were disciplined for pencils
chewed in boredom.
Now, sounds of gnawing wood
were ignored. The doctor knew
that it could be the only thing
they would have to eat that day.

Without Rest

*"It has been a long time since I have blessed the world.
I tried to tonight. It didn't work." – Janusz Korczak*

With eyes that rebuked sleep,
the doctor peered over
the piles of sleeping rags.

The dust-frosted window
framed the ghetto's stove--
the weather, a cold oven,
baked a pan of water the
day before. The children's
heavy slumber breaths
dripped off the walls.

Last night's journal pages
floated in a smeared cloud,
the paper thicker than the roof.

No glow echoed
through the window--
the moon extinguished
since occupation began.

A young boy rolled over,
opened his swollen
shadowed eyes, and
watched Korczak think
from across the room.

Sleep

"Loneliness does not hurt. I value memories." – Janusz Korczak

For the first time,
the doctor fell asleep
while the children
tossed in their cots.

Tonight, he refused to listen
to their muffled moans.
They were his children but
they were not his memories.

Korczak had been in bed
for the past two days.
His mother never strayed
far from the bedroom lintel.
His father stopped in irregularly,
as fathers will do, forcing him
to sit up or walk around
to get the fever out of his system.

On the third day Korczak's
mind returned from its trip.
Before he could sit up in bed
his father walked into the room,
dropped a set of clothes on his lap
and said, "Get up!
It's time to go for a walk."

The doctor could still taste
the soda ice and pineapple juice
when he reached for a piece of paper.
In a blurry half-sleep he wrote:

*"I feel old whenever I
reminisce about the past,
the bygone years and events.
I want to be young,
so I make plans for the future."*

He knew they could no longer make plans.

Warsaw Epidemic

"I used to write at stops, in a meadow under a pine tree, sitting on a stump. Everything seemed important and if I did not note it down I would forget. An irretrievable loss to humanity." – Janusz Korczak

The sun peeled the
gray from clouds,
burning their pewter lining.

Mid-day February and
sick students were having
troubled afternoon naps.
Their dry heaves echoed
in the doctor's ears-- he had
nothing to cure a cough,
no antidote for a fever.
The flu flooded the ghetto
like a forgotten fog.

The children lay tightly
curled in their cots-- they
lay pale, restlessly immobile.
With every turning groan,
their clothes ruffled like wet paper.

Some orphans cried but
nobody made a sound.
Many prayers are silent.

Below the venting glass
panes, standing on the sleet
encrusted sidewalk, soldiers
laughed while slurping soup-
Korczak's stomach twisted
as he heard uneaten broth
splash and sizzle in the snow.

The fragrant steam slid
through cracked windows;
he listened as his children
sniffed and moaned. He had
no bowls to scrape with
spoons they did not possess.

Door to Door and Back

"The children are living in constant uncertainty, in fear." – Janusz Korczak

He slid through the hallway
on the soles of his blistered feet,
ignoring the usual volunteers.
It was the cracks, like veins in
forest green and gray marble,

that reminded the doctor of why
he left every day to collect donations--
like the children the cracks
grew both higher and deeper.

Korczak eased down the stairs.
The reality of the railing was that
each time he leaned on it
for support it became looser--
without reinforcements it would break.

Slightly winded from his descent,
the doctor approached the fragile
Krochmalna Street door and listened.

Once the muffled clicking
of an officer's shoes passed,
he grasped his thinning coat,
braced himself for the
hypothermic Warsaw winter,
and walked into stinging snow.

Drifts muted his footsteps,
silence enveloped the ghetto--
as soundless as a still clapper.
Not a single ringing coin
echoed in the hush--
each mother had her
own children to sustain.

Cracks in the wall had grown
by the time the doctor returned.
He had nothing to fill them.

Without His Mother to Light the Candles

"Two o'clock in the morning. Silence." – Janusz Korczak

The violin slid through his fingers,
singing through every shaking note.
The bow frayed under his bony hand
while the strings pitched and swayed
across the paper's faded bars.

He played every night
through the span of a candle.

Melting light rolled down the stem and
swept across the table; he began to weep.
Once the wax dripped off the edge and
onto his bare knee, the tears ceased,
the music stopped; his voice whispered,
"Shalom."

Children's Games

*"Everything else has its limits, only brazen shamelessness is limitless...
I wish I had nothing, so that they might see it for themselves, and that
would be that." – Janusz Korczak*

Playing jacks was all she would do.
Every day.

Occasionally the doctor
would step on a jack. He
always picked them up
and returned them to
the little girl. Every time,
he noticed her hands seemed
colder than the pointed metal.

She gradually lost them all
despite his efforts to find them.
Small rocks from gutters
proved to be adequate substitutes--
they were easier on feet as well.

When she lost the pink rubber ball,
the only thing for her to do was sleep.
The guard knew what he was doing.

A Hundred Stars

"People are naïve and good-hearted. And probably unhappy."- Janusz Korczak

He strolled through
sidewalk slush to
collect donations used
to support his children;
they were contributions
needed to prevent his Jews
from being forgotten.

With his daily persistence, he
eagerly received tattered marks
from ghetto inmates without
concern for his reputation;
this is what King Matthew
would have done.

At night, by the light
of a hundred blue stars glowing
from frayed threads wrapped
around the sleeping children,
he would write in his journal
with a pencil sharpened at both ends.

This was his lull of huddled peace
when he could record,
not yet a Kaddish for his children,
rather a prayer: to be able
to live through another day.
By morning, his smudged plea
had faded from the page.
Ink was precious--
its permanence was reserved
for lists marked by the SS.

Beyond the orphanage,
the only people who knew
the names of his flock
wore swastikas
stamped on their sleeves.
So long as his children
were carried on a clipboard
titled "Treblinka" he would
never let the executioner's pen
forget the name Korczak.

The Assistant's Diary: August 4th, 1942

"For in the hour of reckoning I am not inside a solitary cell of the saddest hospital in the world but surrounded by butterflies and grasshoppers, and I can hear a concert of crickets and a soloist high up in the sky- the skylark." – Janusz Korczak

The doctor has been writing fewer pages
as the calendar has pared its months.
What was once an opus of aspirations
has become a ghetto diary--
recording occurrences of the day.

His thoughts are becoming weak.
The eloquent script used to pen
A Child's Right to Respect
is now a collection of
abandoned words-- he knows
his energy can no longer
be wasted on literary devices.

I see the doctor has finished for tonight.
I hope to get them done quickly
so I may also sleep.

Amidst the children's
cacophony of coughs,
the typewriter keys popped
with every staggered finger stroke
like moist maple wood in a flame.

These are the last words
the ink embossed on the page:

"What would he do if I nodded to him? Waved my hand in a friendly gesture?

"Perhaps he doesn't even know that things are- as they are?

"He may have arrived only yesterday, from far away..."

With His Children

"The world knows nothing of many great Poles."- Janusz Korczak

Some children high stepped, others
had to be dragged by their armbands,
but most of them, free
from the crucible orphanage walls,
blindly obeyed the doctor.

"They don't want you, just the children!"

He never replied to the pleading few.
He only broke step twice with his troop--
the first was to make sure the children followed;
the second was to hand a stack of papers
to a coughing soot-haired youth-- the
one child in the crowd that day not being
forced to march. Then, the doctor
resumed his pace as caboose of the line.

The ghetto sea thinned as the
hazy box car opened its doors--
for every child that entered the train,
ten people lost their voices.

When the doctor was the only one left
to walk through the sliding doors,
the solitary thing that could be heard
was the ticking of a pocket watch
lying in the corner of the cattle car.

Tick! Tick! Tick!

The Last Sign of God in the World

"Now that every day brings so many strange and sinister experiences and sensations I have completely ceased to dream." – Janusz Korczak

Below the smokestack sky
the rose pressed up from under
the concrete Treblinka wall.
It was the only color seen
from the crowded cattle car.

Korczak followed his pupils'
dry eyes as they passed
the flower and entered the camp.

The petals haunted the doctor.
They were the same red
he had seen dripping from
the children's chapped hands.

Janusz knew the rose was
the same red as the fire that
caused hundreds of mothers
to fall on the heads of sons
and daughters they never knew.

The train stopped, the doors
opened, and the doctor led
his students into the cold
smoldering courtyard. As
his young Jews huddled and
clamped around his waist,
the crimson rose
continued to haunt his eyes.

A Pure Breath

"What matters is that all this did happen." – Janusz Korczak

The boy pushed away sleep and,
blinking his silent eyes in the candlelight,
he listened to Korczak's voice.

Echoing above the soldier's
ash-muffled steps, the only
sound in the camp was
the doctor's paper cracking
like a stiff flag in a sharp
breeze as he chiseled lead
onto what once was white.

Despite his arthritic fingers,
he had written hundreds of
pages in the ghetto;
but these were the first
curled letters of his Kaddish.
This was his last leaf of script;
the last journal entry which
would never leave his hand.

This was his voice that would rain
down with his body and
rest in the lungs of Treblinka.

III

Filip Müller

Rachmones I

"We had been running for about 100 metres, when a strange flat-roofed building loomed up before us." – Filip Müller

In the distance, with the air
above the stacks still,
ovens stood in industrial
innocence within their brick
and mortar womb.

The furnace lay cold and gray
with its cast iron door swung open,
and waited to receive the next Jew –
to embrace them in its crucible heart.

In silent slavery and in slumber
the bodies kept flowing past
Filip like a swollen stream.

Ice and snow singed his feet.
The inhumanity of the inanimate.

Job

"I was like one hypnotized and obeyed each order implicitly. Fear of more blows, the ghastly sight of piled-up corpses, the biting smoke, the humming of fans and the flickering of flames, the whole infernal chaos had paralysed my sense of orientation as well as my ability to think." – Filip Müller

The wooden doors slid to the right
and unnumbered inmates were
forced in to the mass of humanity.

The fire hose hissed as droplets
fell and froze to their lips.

They patiently shuffled their feet
across sheets of crystallized tears.

Their clothes stiff with icy sweat.

The able bodied were embroidered
with needled ink. Their numbers
stripped them of nearly everything,
leaving only that which damned them:
their blood and their faith.

Filip was chosen to live;
chosen to watch others die;
chosen to stay warm on
the coldest days as families,
towns, and villages were
reduced to smoke and ash.

His breath choked thick
with the tribes and lineage
of every Jew. This was a test
Job was never forced to endure.

Rachmones II

"Behind it a round red-brick chimney rose up into the sky." – Filip Müller

The handle sizzled in
his snow chapped palm.

As he pulled the furnace door
he could hear the air caress
the ashen body within.

He paused. The bitter taste
of parched flesh
seized his muscles.

The guard turned and began
a slow walk in Filip's direction.
In his eyes, sinister delight
glowed brighter as he inched
toward 'his' inmate.

His neck bulged as his arm
rose and his fist clenched.
Filip pulled the iron door open
but he could not avoid the assault.

Sabbath Gassing

"I went to the pillar near which the girls had talked to me. There I found the girl Yana who had asked me to take off her necklace and give it to her lover as a last keepsake. She lay where she had said she would. I took off the necklace, pocketed it and left the room." – Filip Müller

They walked through the doors
with their right hands raised
looking to brush their kissed fingers
against the mezuzah that was not there.

The showers were used in solitude.
No guards in the room.
This was their time to destroy silence.

The sun set with the
latching of the double doors.

The Sabbath greetings began.
"Shabbat Shalom!"
Voices repeated,
muting the constant echoes.

The dialogue ceased as
the air became thick and
their bodies remained dry.

The pipes did not
flush with water –
they hissed with gas
as the screaming began.

Rachmones III

"It took some time before I began to realize that there were people lying there at my feet who had been killed only a short while before." – Filip Müller

Their pressed uniforms
stood out like blood on
a veined marble head stone.
The ash and snow mixed
under their feet. Each soldier
weighed more than two
or three prisoners combined.

Tissue stretched taut between
bones – he no longer knew
how people could still be alive.
The line between life
and death began to fray.

Singed with the scent of silence.
Pink skin now gray ash.
The smell of blackened flesh
turned his barren stomach.

After months of touching
the hands of the dead
he began to envy those
he saw gasping for air.
He wished it would be over.

He could no longer remember
what fresh air tasted like.
The air would forever remain
dry and thick in his lungs –
this is what it is like to taste sorrow.

Haunted by the whispers only
G-d was meant to hear.

When he was younger,
he used to be afraid
to go to sleep; now
he was afraid to wake up.

Bar Mitzvah

"Our life of isolation continued. For, although we did not realize this at first, we had become privy to a secret and were no longer allowed to come into contact with other prisoners or with SS men not in the know. That was why we no longer attended roll-call." – Filip Müller

In the illuminated darkness two
candles sizzled in the humid air
struggling to maintain their flame.

The youngest girl in the room
stood watch by the window
to make sure that silence
was all the guards could hear.

David hunched over his Torah portion
trying to remember the rhythm of the chant.

He shivered as his voice
quivered his whispers.
Slowly, the Hebrew
was liberated from his lips.

The Rabbi stood and shook his hand
welcoming him as part
of the shrinking minyan.

Filip listened from across the camp
as shouts of "Mazel Tov" echoed
from one building to another
as the guards turned their heads
in the direction of the celebration.
Some troops smiled and enjoyed
the rare moment of happiness
while others grinned knowing
they would all be quiet soon enough.

Baruch Hashem

"Even before the bottom bar had been unbolted both wings of the double doors were bulging to the outside under the weight of the bodies." – Filip Müller

The Hasidim seemed to stroll
from the crammed cattle cars.
The black dressed crowd was three,
if not four, generations deep.
They walked knowing what
was going to happen but without
any final words passed from
father to son or from son to father.
Their last words were reserved
for G-d, "Baruch Hashem."

Two brief words repeated
every three steps – stated simply
without anger or fear or hatred or
remorse to quiver their voices.
The only audible emotion was relief.

Filip watched in disbelief as these
learned and faithful men walked
with deliberate steps; following
orders without having to be told twice.
Their somber gait announced
the knowledge of their fate.

The men disappeared as Filip
sealed the gas chamber door.

The hissing pipes rattled and
screaming coughs commenced.
Echoes faded to faithful whispers
giving way to last exhaled
gasps which rang in Filip's ears.

He broke the seal to the chamber and
continued the work that gave him breath
but took away his life. It took thirty
minutes to clear the mounds
of humanity pressing their lips
to the door for one last breath.

There was not a single body
in these mangled mounds
which was not bruised, scraped,
cut, crushed, or broken. But now
they lay without pain or pulse.

Once the last of these piles had been
removed, Filip peered into the shattered
room. Near the middle generations
of Hasidim lay on their backs with
their faces, calm and clean,
peacefully facing G-d.

Nazi Gold Rush

"One evening towards the end of October I went on night duty as one of a team of 100 prisoners. Together with another few experienced prisoners I was picked for this team by Kapo Kaminsky and instructed to organize valuables, if possible." – Filip Müller

No one objected to contributing
to the Nazi gold rush.

The metal table remained unscrubbed –
thousands of stains the same crimson color.

Every body was mined – some held
nothing while others held fillings of gold.
These precious metals were
pried from behind limp lips.

Once all extractions were made,
the nuggets were sent
to be melted in a crucible
while the flesh was retrieved
to be burned in the furnace.

Filip lifted the countless bodies
from the table. The cold blood,
now more purple than red,
dripped from his stained fingers
and rolled slowly down the drain
in the center of the slab.

Disgraced in death and abused in life –
Filip slowly and meticulously
repeated Kaddish for these people –
these people who had no evidence
of torture during their lives or after death.

The only proof of their existence
was the effect they had on others
and the testimony of those
who witnessed their life... and death.

Their body and blood was
property to their murderers but
their faith and dedication was
a gift to G-d and every other Jew.
Yes, they did exist.

The Dead Elders

"The damp stench of dead bodies and a cloud of stifling, biting smoke surged out toward us." – Filip Müller

Wilting under the Sunday snow,
Filip choked on the dry gray –
his parched lungs longed
to feel humidity in the heat.

Filip had been burning evidence
for a week when "the secret" was
exposed to his skin. The elders
were the only ones refreshed
by the gray and pink flesh – seniority
determined by their time at Auschwitz.

Anyone over a year old was
considered close to death – only
ten elders indulged in the secret.
By the time Filip reached
six months old he held a place of
honor as a well established elder.

Filip would grasp the handle and,
with a quick twist and pull,
expose the boiling body within.
Despite the gagging stench,
the humidity of blood, muscle, and fat
moistened their eyes, lips, and lungs.

This was the only way they knew how
a crematoria worker could give back,
give life, give comfort, to his fellow
workers and inmates and family.

The Prayers of a Mussulman

"Now, when I watched my fellow countrymen walk into the gas chamber, brave, proud and determined, I asked myself what sort of life it would be for me in the unlikely event of my getting out of the camp alive. What would await me if I returned to my native town?" – Filip Müller

In the haze of July smoke
the screams seemed silent
as voices strained to swim
through the humidity.

The words of stained dialect
remained clear in the ears
of Filip's head as he lay
recovering from slumber.

His own words pierced the echoes,
"G-d, why have you allowed me
to wake? Why am I to work
another day? Why do you allow
your people to die and burn?

Why do I have to be the last
to look into their clouded eyes
as I carry their pink dyed bodies
to the ovens? Why all this?

Rachmones IV

"But what I could not imagine was how so many people could have been killed at one time." – Filip Müller

Would Kaddish be said for those
who passed before his eyes?
Was it his duty to say Kaddish?

He would say Kaddish every evening;
pray for forgiveness every morning;
and ask to die on his way to work.
He lived on the hope that, someday,
his prayers would be answered...
all of them. But when he placed
the bodies in the furnace he knew
that if he did not do it someone else
would have to – for good or bad –
this was his job.

* * * *

The scars on his hands from
the furnace door still carried the smell
of flesh years after Auschwitz.

* * * *

At first he believed G-d had a plan;
then, a plan without G-d; now, G-d
will grant his people life but will not
save the life of each person – he knew
they must save each other and save themselves.

He passed time with hope – maybe
his wife has survived, maybe
his children are still alive – but
the hours felt different. Each
minute had something absent;
each second contained a void.
Somehow he knew his family
was shattered but hope was all
he had and they could not
take that away from him.

Liberation

"It was, incredibly, a complete anti-climax. This moment, on which all my thought and secret wishes had been concentrated for three years, evoked neither gladness nor, for that matter, any other feelings inside me." – Filip Müller

Behind the barbed wire web,
the dead looked more alive than
those who clutched to the fence
with their bruised and bleeding hands.

Rot, feces, ash, and dust
suffocated the stench
of diesel fumes billowing
from the Sherman tanks.

Polish, German, Yiddish,
and Hebrew pleading bled
into the ears of the terrified
and appalled liberators
who could do nothing more
than torture the Jews.

The soldiers searched one another
for any food they could find –
fresh, frozen, or otherwise.
But before the morsels could be
passed to cracked lips
the allied doctors rushed
to barricade the camp saying,
"Too little food and they die!
Too much food and they die!"

Notes

I: Hertha Feiner

1) All quotes used as epigraphs are taken from <u>Before Deportation: Letters from a Mother to Her Daughters: January 1939 – December 1942</u> by Hertha Feiner:

> Feiner, Hertha. <u>Before Deportation: Letters from a Mother to Her Daughters: January 1939 – December 1942</u>. Northwestern University Press: Evanston (IL), 1999.

2) July 1939 was the last time that Inge and Marion visited Hertha.

3) "Mutter" is a German word meaning "Mother". "Mutti" is a diminutive of the German word "Mutter" meaning "Mom" or "Mommy". "Mutterlein" is German for "Little Mother".

4) When Feiner writes "my new work began on Monday at 7:00 A.M." she is referring to her beginning her new job assigned to her by the Nazi's to type the deportation lists. She later makes reference to this job when she states "the list."

5) Kaddish in its original Aramaic form, Kadosh, means 'holy' or 'sanctify'. Mourners (typically, only close family members) first recite the kaddish at the cemetery after the burial. The kaddish is not a prayer about death. It is an affirmation of life and faith in God. It reaffirms the mourner's relationship with God and God's will in this world.

6) "Meshugga le-davar" is a Yiddish phrase meaning "crazy over (or about) one thing."

7) On March 12, 1943, Hertha Feiner committed suicide by swallowing a capsule of potassium cyanide while on a train heading to Auschwitz.

II: Janusz Korczak

8) All quotes used as epigraphs are taken from <u>Ghetto Diary</u> by Janusz Korczak:

> Korczak, Janusz. <u>Ghetto Diary</u>. Yale University Press: New Haven (CT), 2003.

9) King Matthew, in "Teaching His Children" and "A Hundred Stars", was a didactic character created by Korczak to teach the children morals through the use of stories and plays.

10) "The Assistant's Diary: August 4th, 1942" is told from the point of view of one of Korczak's assistants who would type everything that Korczak wrote in his journal. Entries were typed either the same night or the next morning depending when Korczak finished writing. Korczak never mentioned this assistant by name.

11) <u>A Child's Right to Respect</u> was one of Korczak's earlier works, from around the turn of the century, written to educate both parents and teachers.

12) August 4th, 1942 is the date of the last journal entry written by Korczak before being sent to Treblinka.

13) Janusz Korczak was a pen name. Henryk Goldzmit, his original name, was born in Warsaw in 1878 or 1879 (no one is sure of the exact date).

14) <u>Ghetto Diary</u> was not published until 1956, long after Korczak's death at Treblinka.

15) No one from the orphanage, adult or child, lived to see the end of the war.

III: Filip Müller

16) All quotes used as epigraphs are taken from <u>Eyewitness Auschwitz: Three Years in the Gas Chambers</u> by Filip Müller:

> Müller, Filip. <u>Eyewitness Auschwitz: Three Years in the Gas Chambers</u>. Ivan R. Dee Publishers: Chicago (IL), 1999.

17) "Rachmones" is a Yiddish word which means "compassion", involving being able to feel the suffering of others and,

in doing so, nurturing a desire to alleviate that suffering. Simply put, acting in the image of G-d.

18) The "Sonderkommando" was a unit of prisoners assigned to work in the gas chambers and crematoria of Auschwitz.

19) A "mezuzah" is a scroll (containing the Sh'ma prayer) affixed to the door-posts of one's house and the rooms within one's house. The Mezuzah, in its case, is nailed or screwed or glued to the right side of the door, in the upper third part of the door-post, leaning inward towards the interior of the house or the room.

20) "Shabbat Shalom" is a common Hebrew term meaning "Good Sabbath" or "Peaceful Sabbath".

21) The gas chambers of Auschwitz were made to look like showers in order to lure in the inmates. When the chamber was sealed Zyclon B gas was pumped into the room.

22) A side effect of the Zyclon B gas was that it turned the skin pink.

23) A "Bar Mitzvah" is a Hebrew term meaning "Son of the Commandments"; it is the confirmation of a Jewish boy at age 13 into adulthood.

24) A "Minyan" is a quorum of ten Jews (ten men in Orthodox communities) required for praying as a "community," or for the public reading of the Torah, or for reciting the "Kaddish," or other ritual matters of special holiness.

25) "Motzel Tov" is a Hebrew term meaning "good luck"; it is used to express congratulations.

26) "Baruch Hashem" is a Hebrew term meaning "Thank G-d".

27) Hasidim are Ultra-Orthodox Jews.

28) "Nazi Gold Rush". Before cremation of the bodies, the Nazi's ordered that all "valuables" be removed from their possession. This included gold fillings and anything that may have been hidden in the body.

29) "Dead Elders". The prisoners at Auschwitz, the Sonderkommando in particular, formed a hierarchy among

them in accordance with their time in the unit and time in the camps.

30) "Mussulman" was camp slang for an prisoner who had lost the will to live.

31) The Nazi's evacuated Auschwitz in January 1945; the camp was liberated by the allied forces in May 1945.

32) "Too little food and they die! / Too much food and they die!" When the allied forces liberated many of the camps the medics and doctors stopped the soldiers from handing out food. Because the survivors had not been able to eat for so long there was a great risk that they could overeat and rupture their stomach. However, they knew that if they did not give them anything, the survivors would die of starvation.

About The Author

Sean M. Teaford has honed a reputation for creating hauntingly accessible and emotionally unforgettable images in his poetry. Over the past 15 years, Sean has published over 50 poems, articles, and photographs in numerous magazines throughout the United States and the United Kingdom including (but not limited to) *The Endicott Review*, *The Mad Poets Review*, *Poetry Motel*, *Zillah*, *The Aurorean*, *Spare Change*, *Midstream Magazine*, *The Hypertexts*, and others. His work was also included in the revised edition of Charles Fishman's anthology <u>Blood to Remember: American Poets on the Holocaust</u> (Time Being Books, 2008) and has been the subject of numerous reviews and profiles around the world.

A convert to Conservative Judaism, Sean M. Teaford received his M.F.A. in Creative Writing from Rosemont College in Rosemont, Pennsylvania (2008) and his B.A. in English from Endicott College in Beverly, Massachusetts (2005). He was Endicott College's nominee for the 2003, 2004, and 2005 Ruth Lilly Fellowships and won the 2004 Veterans for Peace Poetry Contest. In addition to serving as an editor for a variety of literary publications, including *The Endicott Review* and *The Mad Poets Review*, he has coordinated numerous poetry readings across the Northeast and has been a featured reader in the Boston and Philadelphia areas.

In recent years, Sean has devoted his creative efforts to writing a daily blog, *Time To Keep It Simple*, which has served as his primary outlet for the observations, emotions, and reflections that can be found in the poetry that he still published on occasion. A public relations professional, avid traveler, passionate genealogist, and active mason, Sean lives in Morgantown, Pennsylvania with his wife and young son.